My acci

Jenny Giles
Illustrated by Priscilla Cutter

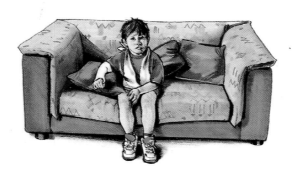

Here I am,
on my skateboard.

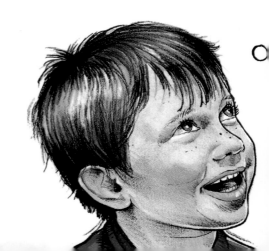

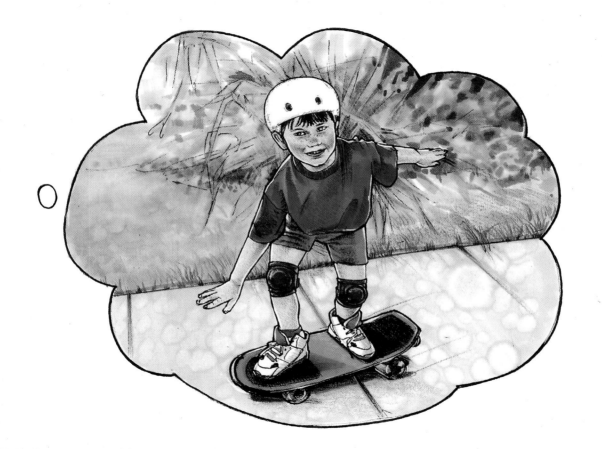

Here I am,
on the ground.

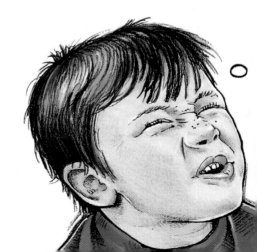

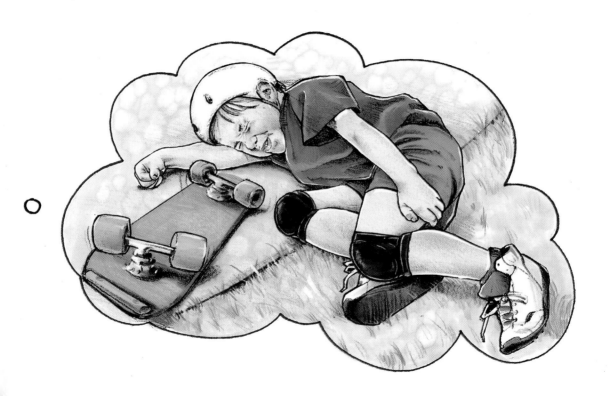

Here I am,

in the ambulance.

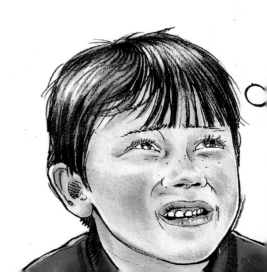

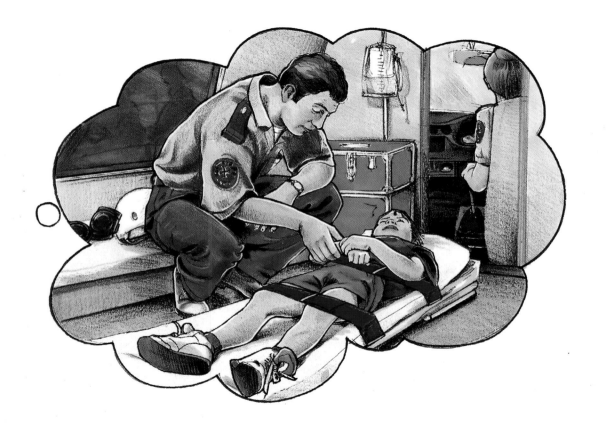

Here I am,
at the hospital.

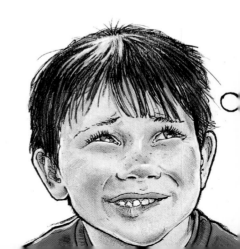

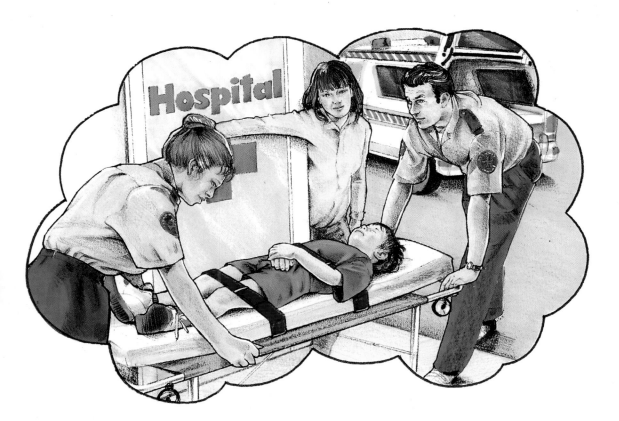

Here I am,

in the X-ray room.

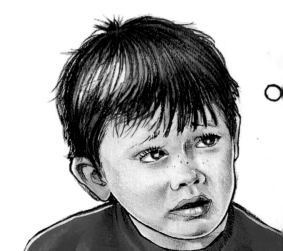

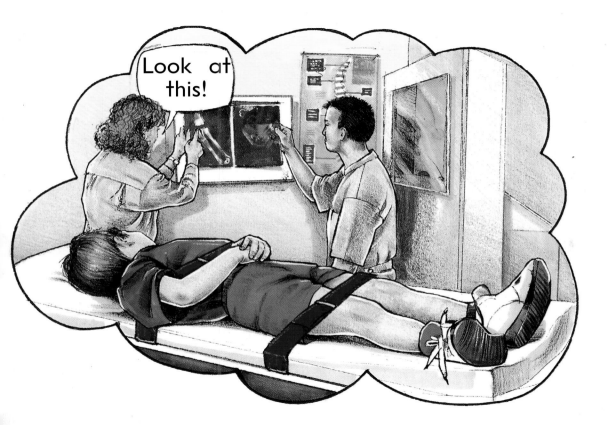

Here I am,

in the cast room.

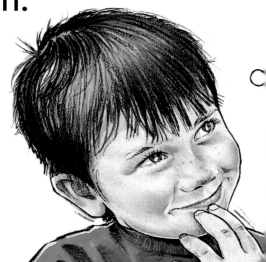

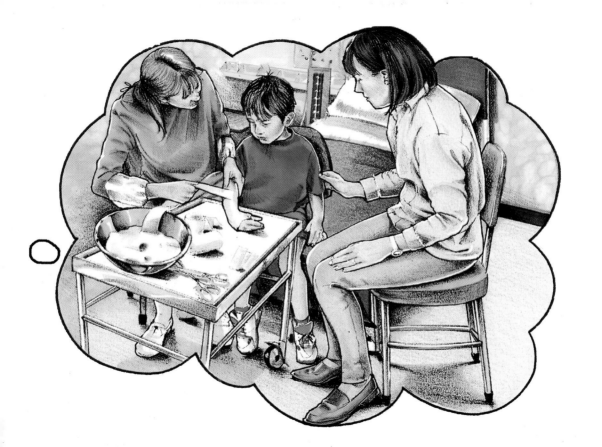

Here I am,

at home.

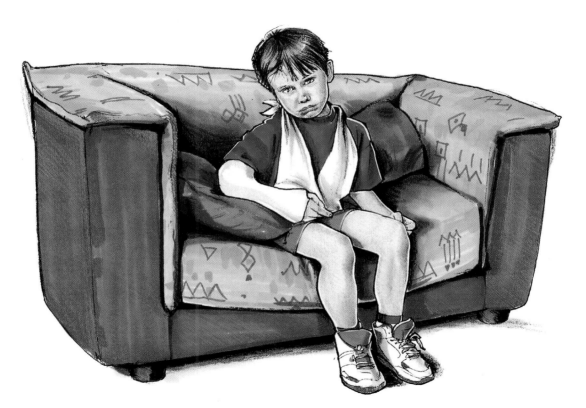

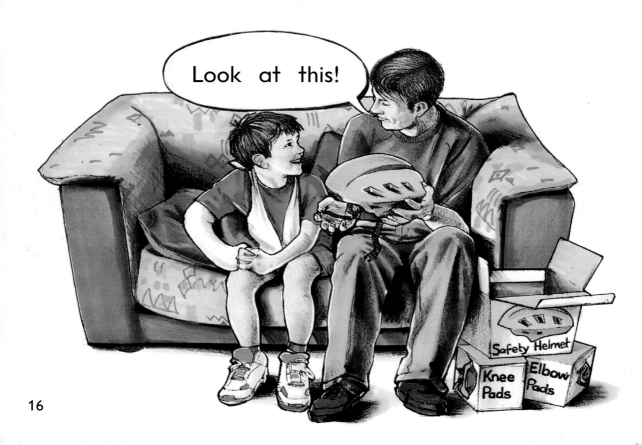